It's Not Easy Being a Mom

JOYCE MATANGA

Copyright © 2024 by Joyce Matanga

No part of this book may be reproduced in any form or by any electronic or mechanical means, including information storage and retrieval systems, without written permission from the author, except for the use of brief quotations in a book review.

Scriptures taken from the Holy Bible, New International Version®, NIV®. Copyright © 1973, 1978, 1984, 2011 by Biblica, Inc.™ Used by permission of Zondervan. All rights reserved worldwide. www.zondervan.com The "NIV" and "New International Version" are trademarks registered in the United States Patent and Trademark Office by Biblica, Inc.™

Cover Design and Formatting by RLS Creativity
https://qr.link/7lkNPU

Paperback: 978-1-7382403-2-6

E-Book: 978-1-7382403-3-3

Photos provided by Joyce Matanga

This book is dedicated to my children: Melody, Purity, and Lumbweni. I had this passion to write to my children to show them how difficult it is to care for your children when you must leave them home and go to work in order to earn an income.

Contents

Introduction vii

1. What is Motherhood? — 1
2. What is God's View of Motherhood? — 3
3. What Are the Struggles of Mothers? — 5
4. Dealing with Guilty Feelings — 7
5. Finding Quality Care For Your Child While At Work — 9
6. Making Difficult Choices — 11
7. Coping With Emotions — 13
8. An Introduction to Daily Affirmations — 15
9. How to Make Daily Affirmations — 17
10. Do Babies Know Who Their Parents Are? — 19
11. Does the Baby Know the Babysitter? — 21
12. Do Babies Know When the Mother is Not Around? — 23
13. My Lessons in Childcare — 25
14. Praying As a Mother — 27
15. Negative Things in Children — 29
16. How Do You Break Negative Things in Children? — 31

17. Do You View Babysitting as Challenging for Your Babysitter? 33
18. Communication Between Your Babysitter and Yourself 35
19. Do You Know the Struggles that are There Between You and Your Babysitter? 37
20. Conclusion 39

Acknowledgments 41
About the Author 43
Also by Joyce Matanga 45

Introduction

Just after my baby was born the midwife handed the baby to me and placed her on my tummy for skin-to-skin contact. This is a good way to say hello to this amazing gift in your life. The baby will start attaching and begin the process of learning and growing.

As months go by, depending on the country where you are, you may need support with your child when you return to work. This is where you engage a babysitter or you find a childcare facility for your baby. When my children were three months old, I had to leave them home with different baby care-givers in my country. I am thankful to God for providing me with the women who cared for my children while I went to work.

INTRODUCTION

Happy and successful motherhood is fulfilled when we involve God in every step we take. Many mothers go through motherhood behind closed doors, feeling frustrated, feeling lonely, and wanting to quit their jobs.

This book is a mixture of my own experience as a young mother, communicated experience and again my experience now that I am older.

I wrote this book for young mothers and working mothers in relation to the struggles that I went through as a mother. My prayer is you find God's presence and protection as you raise your child, with or without other help. May your insecurities be broken in Jesus name.

May you experience that God's presence goes with you to work and also remains with your child at home. Motherhood is not easy, but God will provide everything you need to be the mother He has called you to be.

CHAPTER 1
What is Motherhood?

Motherhood is selfless and calls for a lot of sacrifices for the children.

These sacrifices start from conception till the child is born and then continue. A mother works very hard making sure the child is fed, equipped with knowledge, skills, and abilities to make him or her a competent human being.

I never thought so much about children when I was young. In my growing years, I never used to love and play like a mum and I remember my mother having noticed that. She would make comments like, "Joyce is not very passionate about children."

CHAPTER 2
What is God's View of Motherhood?

Motherhood from God's perspective is about nurturing life. God created and equipped women to nurture the life He created both biologically and spiritually. So as mothers we nurture children and often friends help us on the journey of motherhood.

> ISAIAH 66:13 NIV: "As a mother comforts her child, so will I comfort you and you will be comforted over Jerusalem."

I am amazed to see how my heart was naturally turned to the needs of my children during my life as a mother and I have learnt that God views mothers as He sees us in relation to Him. This is amazing.

CHAPTER 3

What Are the Struggles of Mothers?

Before I became a mother, I did not realize the struggles that a mother goes through. I looked at my mother who had 10 of us as her children and she was always wanting to do the best for us.

It is when I became a mother in the mid 1990's that I saw the responsibilities that came with being a mother as well as when I became a grandmother in my fifties. I have come to learn as I meet people in the community that many mothers find themselves struggling to manage time and childcare while trying to keep up with life.

Becoming a mother and working as a mother and also helping with childcare has transformed my life and developed within me a compassionate love for young mothers. I will talk about the common struggles of motherhood in this book.

On the positive side, we all know motherhood brings joy, but we often do not realize the battles that go on behind closed doors until we become a young mother, a single mother, or a new person in a new country. If we could see the emotional stress, we would be compelled to pray for these women. But we know one thing. God sees you and cares for you more than anyone.

CHAPTER 4

Dealing with Guilty Feelings

During my first months of returning to work I felt so guilty leaving my three-month-old baby with a stranger and I think most mothers feel this. Behind the curtains at the hospital, I have heard women say, "If I was a billionaire, I would not leave my baby."

But this is life as many mothers experience it, so how do we fight this guilt? Learn to apply the word of God:

"Do not be anxious about anything, but in every situation, by prayer and petition, with thanksgiving, present your requests to God. And the peace of God, which transcends all understanding, will guard your hearts and your minds in Christ Jesus," (Philippians 4:6-7 NIV).

CHAPTER 5
Finding Quality Care For Your Child While At Work

As a first time mom, it is important to look at each phase of motherhood and check the things and qualities you will look for when employing a baby care provider. You will need someone with patience. Someone who understands and enjoys children. You will also need someone with creativity, flexibility, and good decision-making skills.

Looking for a baby care provider requires praying on your part as a mother for God to help you. I recall those days when I knew I should be going to work and the person I hired did not show up or sent a friend saying she was sick or no longer wanted to work for me.

Going to work and leaving your baby at a daycare or home with relatives is a struggle for a mother's heart. "Has my baby eaten? Is my baby fine?"

Mothers do not just feel guilty about leaving children home. They may also feel bad for not helping their parents and they may feel embarrassed to tell co-workers or friends about how stressed they may be over leaving their child at home.

I recall when I had my first-born child. I left her with the baby care provider and went to work. I do not know what happened. My husband decided to go back home and found the baby care provider had left our baby in a tub with water. My husband had to grab the baby out and we had to start looking for someone else to come in. It was not a good experience.

Coming from a third-world country, I remember employing young girls with no training to care for my child. But God kept my children safe. Is God not God? He is. We can overcome this guilt by praying about it, doing our best, and being good to others. We can also practise kindness with the people we meet or work with.

CHAPTER 6

Making Difficult Choices

As a mother we need to make some difficult choices. One of the most challenging problems is to make choices between outings with friends and spending time with your baby.

I struggled with feelings of guilt over trying to achieve effective work. I also struggled mentally —is this worthy doing? I often asked myself, "Am I being a good mother?"

Sometimes even finding time to eat, you need to choose between a healthy meal or just an ice cream when time to cook is not there. A nursing mother needs to eat even healthier than any other woman. Eating breakfast, lunch, and supper is very important. With the struggles in housework and baby care, I struggled to eat healthy meals, but I tried. I found the more I tried to eat well, the more weight I gained. However, for the sake of my baby, I chose to eat healthy meals and let my baby get the nutrients from my breast milk.

CHAPTER 7

Coping With Emotions

Being a mother can be emotionally draining as you feel pulled in all directions. You are thinking about the needs of your husband, your child, and the entire family. Whoops! This often feels like it is too much to handle.

During my early motherhood I found these tips helpful:

- It is important to find support from your family, friends, and colleagues.
- Find moms to pray with once a week. You can do this in person, or on the phone. There are many options with new technology.

- Find a flexible work arrangement. Discuss your needs with your employer. Don't be afraid.

CHAPTER 8

An Introduction to Daily Affirmations

Daily affirmations are very important. I learnt about daily affirmations from the church I attended in Zambia as a young mother. Praise God I was involved in the intercession ministry and we learnt to pray for our children. I remember going to prayer meetings every week on Friday when I was not working. I am not saying I have stopped. No, I still go for prayers here in Canada every Wednesday at our church. I love making affirmations.

Affirmations are statements that you repeat and affirm...positive beliefs you state with confidence about your child. Let us talk about a negative character quality and make a positive affirmation. If we pay attention we can see,

"Wow, this happened once. Then it happened again, and it continued happening repeatedly. In fact, it is still happening."

I knew a child (not of my own) who had difficulties reading. I started to address this negative and apply the Word of God and speak His Word upon this child. I have seen things turn around. This child has been amazing. She now lives a very positive and productive life.

CHAPTER 9
How to Make Daily Affirmations

The Bible is full of affirmations and this is the model we can use for our daily affirmations for our children. To help your children change from those negatives, you will find affirmations in the Word of God.

For example you can say:

- I affirm my child is turning to your word, God.
- I affirm my child will not turn away from your word.
- I affirm what you have said about your plan for this child that it will come to pass.

- I affirm in class she shall be the head and not the tail.

Make statements about her being successful. Dear mother, there is no better place for getting affirmations than the Bible. Read from Genesis to Revelation and find affirmations suitable for your child. I discovered these affirmations work. They are still working for my children in their adult lives.

FOR PRAYER AND COUNSELLING, reach out to your local church or you can leave me a message on my Facebook Page: https://www.facebook.com/joyce.matanga.

CHAPTER 10
Do Babies Know Who Their Parents Are?

Your baby is so special! A baby's ability to smell begins in the womb when it can smell the amniotic fluid. Have you noticed a few weeks after a baby is born it can differentiate between the mother's smell and a stranger?

At three months the baby smiles at the mother. At four months it will turn to the mother and expect her to respond. Then at seven months it will start to respond to the mother's anger, stress, and strangers. So, the baby knows his mum.

CHAPTER 11

Does the Baby Know the Babysitter?

I have learned that babies form strong attachments to multiple caregivers including their mothers and babysitters. A baby knows who their mom is and who their babysitter is.

CHAPTER 12

Do Babies Know When the Mother is Not Around?

Between four to seven months of age babies develop a sense of object permanence. That means they realize objects and people exist, even when they can't see them. They realize that mum goes out and comes back, and they also know they are taken to daycare and brought back at the end of the day. Babies express anxiety by crying when you leave them or when Dad leaves.

CHAPTER 13
My Lessons in Childcare

You won't believe this, but it's true. Children and babies usually develop a secure attachment to the primary caregiver. This will impact how they will react to relationships with others. I found this when caring for my grandchild—we both became attached to each other. I started loving her more.

Now think of the person providing baby care who you do not know. This calls for you as the mom to learn to break any negative things the child may inherit from those who look after them when you are away. (For more information, go to Chapter Sixteen: How Do You Break Negative Things in Children?)

CHAPTER 14

Praying As a Mother

As mothers it is important to pray to God. We should always pray for our children, asking God to bless them. When we pray in faith, our prayers are a support for our children. Never cease to pray for your children.

There are women in the Bible who prayed and I love reading about these women:

- Hannah, mother of Samuel (1 Samuel 1:10-17)
- Sara praying into her old age (Genesis 21)
- Elizabeth (Luke 1)
- Anna the prophetess (Luke 2:36-38).

CHAPTER 15
Negative Things in Children

Children start to show negative things as early as the toddler age and continue into adulthood.

Toddlers and young children tend to have tantrums and break rules. As their social life continues to develop, they will also express these through emotions. Some emotions are negative and some are positive. We are looking at the negative emotions because if not corrected they can became big problems in the future. Let us look at Ephesians 4:14 NIV.

> "So that we no longer be children tossed to and fro by the waves and carried about by every wind of doctrine, by human cunning, by craftiness in deceitful schemes."

This verse is talking about Christians but I love to apply it to children. If not corrected they can fall into these things.

I recall in my parent life seeing negative things in my children and I started to pray for these things. Thank God, I do not see these negatives when they are grown. My daughters are lovely girls. Praise God!

CHAPTER 16

How Do You Break Negative Things in Children?

Breaking negative things in your children is a continuous process. It is a battle. Mothers, we have to fight for our children in prayer. do not be a sleeping mother! Awaken and pray to see the negatives. Then create prayer points and take them to God.

Sometimes we become anxious of the negatives we see in our children. I would say, "Pray dear woman. Pray dear mother. You are not alone. Your child has God to change those negatives. God changed the negatives in my children, and He will do the same for you.

PRAYER TO BREAK NEGATIVE PATTERNS:

Dear God,

I bring baby Chubo (insert the name of your child here) to you. Chubo has so many tantrums...slamming doors, running away when corrected, getting very annoyed. (Replace this with the negative patterns you see in your own child.)

I bring these negative patterns to you and ask you to break them. I am asking you God to perfect him in his journey of life. AMEN

NOTE THAT THIS IS A JOURNEY OF BREAKING NEGATIVES: It does not end after one prayer. We continue to pray. Of course we will be seeing positive changes over time. This is a praise item. Do not forget to thank GOD!

CHAPTER 17

Do You View Babysitting as Challenging for Your Babysitter?

Babysitting is actually challenging and demanding for a babysitter as well as a mom. Do we usually think of the emotional stress a babysitter might have gone through? Often as mothers we complain about the babysitter. Instead, at this particular time, take time to pray for all those taking care of children.

PRAYER:

Dear God,

Thank for this daycare my child goes to. Thank for the staff. Thank for this babysitter for (name of your child).

I ask that you place your protection over my child(ren). I pray you give strength to my babysitter. Show her how much you love her and help me to be thankful for her.

In Jesus' name,

Amen.

CHAPTER 18

Communication Between Your Babysitter and Yourself

I have learned we need to communicate with our babysitters about our child:

- Her eating
- Her dislikes
- What we want done for the baby like toileting, learning, playing, naps, bathing
- Everything we do that works for us as mothers.

I think I need God to forgive me for the way I handled my babysitters in my position as an employer.

CHAPTER 19

Do You Know the Struggles that are There Between You and Your Babysitter?

This is how we create barriers between ourselves and babysitters. There can be a scenario where babysitters are overlooked. We need to recognize that they may also have burnout. They also need stress maintenance. How do you help your babysitter in this area?

1. Pray for her.
2. Allow her to express her challenges.
3. Talk also about your challenges.
4. Discuss and come to an agreement on how things can be done better.

CHAPTER 20
Conclusion

Motherhood is a blessing but let us not ignore the challenges. Let us remember to pray for one another and our children.

God bless and do not forget to make daily affirmations for your children.

Acknowledgments

Thanks to Cecilia Chanda, my young sister's daughter, who allowed me to use her photos. She is currently studying to be a Registered Nurse in Zambia, now in her 3rd year. She testifies, "It has been very hard to find a suitable babysitter to care for my children but God has been faithful."

My sharing and encouragement while I wrote *It's Not Easy Being a Mom* has helped her.

About the Author

Joyce Matanga got born again by accepting God's gift of salvation by faith in 1987. She completed grade 12 and then proceeded to nursing college. She got married and still went back to train as a midwife.

Joyce has developed a passion for young mothers. She was also very involved in the ladies' ministry at Agape Christian Centre in Chilialbombwe on the copperbelt province in Zambia.

Joyce now resides in Regina, Saskatchewan, Canada. She testifies that she has seen God's faithfulness in bringing her children up. It was not easy, especially one day when her babysitter decided to leave her baby in a tub full of water. Her challenging experiences have drawn Joyce to write this book.

She is inspired by the word of God and prayer.

Also by Joyce Matanga

Courage for Daily Life: 30 Day Devotional

Are you struggling with fear and discouragement? *Courage for Daily Life* provides bite-sized doses of encouragement and strength.

In this devotional, Joyce Matanga provides:

- **Scriptures** about God's presence
- **Questions** to ponder
- **Personal application**
- **Prayer** for the day

Every believer faces battles. You can march into the war with courage. Allow this gem to equip you for victory.

Start living your best life.

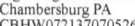

www.ingramcontent.com/pod-product-compliance
Lightning Source LLC
Chambersburg PA
CBHW072137070526
44585CB00016B/1723